Beneath My Wings

A Poetry Collection

Beneath My Wings
A Poetry Collection

Anna-Stina Johansson

This book is dedicated to my family and my true friend.

Copyright Notice

Beneath My Wings A Poetry Collection © 2015, Anna-Stina Johansson

Edited by Jennifer Anderson

Cover Design by Anna-Stina Johansson

Publisher: The Storyteller from Lappland

Contact: info@lapplandstoryteller.com

ISBN 978-91-980161-9-2

ALL RIGHTS RESERVED. This book contains material protected under International and Federal Copyright Laws and Treaties. Any unauthorized reprint or use of this material is prohibited. No part of this book may be reproduced or transmitted in any form or by any means, electronic or mechanical, including photocopying, recording, or by any information storage and retrieval system without express written permission from the author.

Contents

A Blanket……………………………………............……9

A Pot of Gold……………………………...……………10

A Ray of Light……………………………......………...11

A Summer Breeze………………………......…………12

Beloved…………………………………………………14

Beneath my Wings……………………………............16

Butterflies…………………………………………....…17

Cope…………………………………………………....19

Dawn…………………………………………………...20

Demons…………………………………………….…..22

Easter Bunny…………………………………………..23

Fairyland…………………………………….............…24

Falling……………………………………….............….26

Feelings……………………………..…………………28

Fighting Nightmares……………..…………………... 30

Gratefulness…………….…………………..............…32

Hang on………………………………………………..33

I'm Lost…………………………………………….......34

5

Jungle	36
Keep your Dreams Alive	37
Let go	38
Live Life to the Fullest	39
My Meadow	41
My Treasure	42
Never-Ending Love	43
Once Upon a Time	44
Pieces of Me	46
Precious	48
Quiet	49
Respect Yourself	50
Standing out from the Crowd	51
Storm	52
The Angel of the Night	54
The Earth	55
The Night	57
There are No Words	59
Thinking of You	61
Thou Shalt Not Kill	62
To Me They are All the Same	63
True Friendship	65

Underneath the Stars……………………………....67

Vacation………………………………………...68

Walking on Clouds……………………………..70

What is Love?..73

Whisper in the Night…………………...................75

Xmas…………………………………….............76

You………………………………………….…..78

Your own Best Friend…………………………..79

Your Special Someone……………………….....80

Zero……………………………………………..81

A Blanket

A blanket is nice and warm
feels like it protects you
protects you from all
all the evil in the world

A blanket is like a thick layer of snow
which protects the ground
protects the ground from the cold
and gives life to all
all the creatures who search
search shelter from the cold

A blanket surround you
surround you with all its warmth
it makes you feel safe
safe from the outer world
a world that can be very cold at times
Then it's good to have a blanket
a blanket
to seek comfort in

A Pot of Gold

When you have someone
someone that listens
over and over
when no one else will
Is like having a pot of gold
because you can feel rich
if you have someone like that

When you have someone
someone to talk to
when you're feeling down
so you almost drown
Is like having a pot of gold
because you can feel lucky
if you have someone like that

When you have someone
someone who understands
when no one else does
Is like having a pot of gold
because you can feel grateful
if you have someone like that

Feel blessed if you have someone
someone who sparkle as bright
as bright as a golden coin
in your life
Because it's like having
A pot of gold

A Ray of Light

What's more beautiful than a ray of light
that makes even the saddest heart bright
A ray of light brings joy and hope
it gives you strength to cope
It lifts you up when you're down
so you don't drown
drown in your tears and heartache
A ray of light gives you a break
a break from all the misery
The light makes the past feel like history
All you have to do
in order to not feel blue
is to put a smile on your face
and the life embrace

Yes, the ray of light is a beautiful thing
like a golden ring
that glisten
Hoping the one will listen
when you tell what's in your heart
so you can get a fresh start
after your time apart
Hoping the one understands your art
and can read between the lines
to see all the signs
Hoping the one understand
and take your hand
to brighten the way
such as the sunbeam lights your day

A Summer Breeze

A summer breeze is soft and warm
so close your eyes and feel
feel how the breeze caress your skin
It reminds you of the feeling
when someone you love touches you
It makes you smile

Open your eyes and see all the flowers that surround you
Flowers that surround you in different colors
and look at all the amazing butterflies that fly above your head
Blue, yellow, white and purple ones
Maybe one lands on your arm
It gives you a tickling feeling
like when you feel fingertips on your skin

Breathe in the summer breeze
Feel how it lifts up even the saddest soul and the darkest heart
It sweeps away all the sorrows for a while
Look at the sun and watch how it slowly sets behind the mountains
and feel its last rays of light
kiss your face goodnight

Remember this before you fall asleep at night
Remember how you watched the butterfly
fly away in the bright summer night
And you looked at heaven and wondered
if this is what heaven feels like
A place with no sorrow and sadness
Just bright sensations of love and beauty
Thinking that being loved by someone who loves

something as pretty as a butterfly
need to be a beautiful thing

Maybe that is what heaven feels like
It must be hard letting go of something so rare and pure
But your time has not come yet
Your time is on earth
to live for the things that matter to you

Remember this before you go to sleep
How the summer breeze magic took away your sorrows for a while
and you felt surrounded by love and beauty
Remember this before you close your eyes
that you never know what tomorrow brings
Maybe it's your turn to see the light at the end of the tunnel
So live now and don't be afraid of being sad
because one day you will be blessed to feel
feel the summer breeze forever

Beloved

You were my love
You were my friend
You were my everything
And now you are gone
gone forever
You have left the earth for a better place
You have moved to the angels now
to the angels in heaven above

But I am still on earth all alone now
My heart is bleeding but I keep breathing
My emotions are such a mess now
I don't think that I can function without you
And now you are gone
gone to another place

My heart is bleeding and so it will
for a long time ahead

Your heart was like a deep ocean
A deep ocean of love
A deep ocean of love so pure
A love so perfect
And that love you sent to me

I truly wish that I could go to you
I know that I would enjoy lying on a cloud
On a big nice, soft, white cloud
just to lie there and daydream and sleep
is something that I would love to do

But I am still here
here on earth
In a place that will be so empty without you

A place where I no longer can seek comfort in your
beautiful eyes

You stood always by my side through good times and bad
times
You were always there for me and now you are gone
The life goes on and my heart is bleeding
because you are no longer here with me
But I console myself with that you will forever be in my
heart
I will never forget you

And I hope that you at least felt a little bit
a little bit of all the love that I felt for you
Because I felt all the love you gave me
and now I hope that you were able to receive
just some of all the warm feelings that I felt for you and still
do

I have many wonderful memories of you
Memories that I will cherish until the day I die
Because you were my love
You were my friend
You were my everything

Beneath My Wings

I want to feel wind
wind beneath my wings
So I can fly
fly like an eagle

I want to be strong
so I can fight
Fight for what's right
and not give in

I want to be brave
so I can reach the stars
Because I want to be happy
and follow my heart

Butterflies

Close your eyes
dream of butterflies
flying above your head
although you're in bed

A butterfly who is yellow
is your new fellow
A butterfly who is blue
reminds you to stay true
A butterfly who is black
think you should fight back
A butterfly who is orange
doesn't want you to be afraid of a challenge
A butterfly who is purple
helps you to not get caught in a vicious circle
A butterfly who is green
makes you feel like a king or a queen
A butterfly who is red
stops the feeling of dread
A butterfly who is brown
keeps you from feeling down
A butterfly who is pink
helps you to think
A butterfly who is white
comes with the light

So keep dreaming
it stops you from screaming
Let the butterflies protect you
and help you get through
all the hardships you run across
Let the butterflies be your boss

then you'll be cheerful
and never fearful

Cope

It's hard to stay strong
when you long
Long so much
for your touch

You feel like a broken sparrow
like you've been shot with an arrow
Left are only hope
because you want to cope

Be smart
listen to your heart
It'll tell you what to do
that is true

Dawn

When darkness is upon you
because of thoughts of the past
that keeps you from living
Know that even the darkest night
is followed by a beautiful dawn

The daybreak's soft light
and the birds' wonderful song
will heal your broken soul
Your heart will mend
when your eyes look up at heaven
and you feel the first sunbeams
sunbeams that kiss your face warm
Your heart and soul
is no longer cold from dark thoughts
Suddenly the sunrise
make you feel alive again

And what's left of the past
are only memories that won't last
because soon they have vanished
They will be replaced
replaced with thoughts of the present
thoughts of light and joy

So when the darkness has a grip on you
Let go
Think of life
that life has something better to offer you
just around the corner
Don't give up
Don't give in
Don't lose faith

Because when it seems the darkest
that's when the dawn is closest

Demons

When all you do
is feel blue
makes you long for death
so you can take your last breath

All day long
you wish to be strong
Struggle to fight the thought
so you don't get caught
caught in the darkness
since all it gives you is sadness

Demons from hell
makes your life a living hell
You wish you had a gun
so you could have some fun
shooting the demons one by one
feels like making a homerun

Everything becomes a vicious circle
you wish you could watch Steve Urkel
so he can make you smile
and forget about the demons for a while

Easter Bunny

It's funny
when you think of the Easter Bunny
is it a he
or a she
who knows
but on it goes

It brings joy
maybe a toy
or candies
or lilies
or a book
If you take a closer look
maybe you can see who it is
but know this

Easter Bunny brings happiness
and love and kindness
that's all you need to know
so perhaps it's better that it doesn't show
who it is that comes with the light
Just know that it wants you to feel bright

Maybe it's better Easter Bunny is a mystery
since it comes with a special delivery
because it's an act of love
Perhaps a dove
whispered in the Bunny's ear
that it should bring joy to your dear

It's funny
when you think of the Easter Bunny
it makes you feel sunny
since you know it brings a gift from your honey

Fairyland

If I could have taken away your pain
I would have
If I could have traveled back in time
I would have
and made all the wrongs right

If I could have used magic
I would have
then I would have waved my wand
and thrown fairy dust in the air
to make all your pain go away

I wish I knew about a portal
then I would have taken you there
because I wish one could go to a fairyland
to forget one's sorrows for a while
I wish one could go there and hide
hide from the cruel world we live in

In the fairyland I would have taken you
taken you to a good witch
And she would have healed you
healed your broken heart
with her powerful magic
In the fairyland everything would be
would be as you wanted it to be

I'm sorry that I don't know about a portal
so I could have taken you to the fairyland
I'm sorry that we can't go there and hide
hide for a while
from the unfair world we live in

I'm sorry that I don't know any good witch
so she could have healed you

I wish that I could have healed you
but all I have are my words
these words that I'm writing to you
I hope they can ease your pain a little bit
If not
I want you to know
know that I'm always there for you

Falling

It feels like I'm falling
falling like a leaf during fall
when it slowly falls from a tree
But before it lands on a bed of other leaves
it's floating around in the air with all its beauty
Until it lies down to rest on the ground
and it slowly starts to molder
Soon it's forgotten

When hope fades away
it gives room for the darkness to take its place instead
Then it feels like you're falling like a leaf
Not knowing what to feel
when you lose touch of what kept you alive
And below is an endless darkness

You fight to hold on
but that big dark hole keeps pulling you down
It's like the darkness have tentacles
that can't wait to grab hold of you

You don't feel alive
and you're not dead
You just keep floating in between
Not knowing what to do
to shake off that feeling of falling

You want to shoo away the darkness
and fight your way back to the top
So you don't fall down and get suffocated by the darkness
But it's hard to shake away that feeling of falling
when you feel numbed from the outer world
And you're caught in between
between the living and the dead

All you see is gray

Suddenly the phone rings
and you're brought back to the living
when you hear a friendly voice who understands
Then hope grows stronger again
and takes control over the darkness
And you realize that you didn't fell
Instead you landed on a bed of light
that helps you to stay in touch
with what that makes you feel alive

Feelings

What shall one do with all the feelings
feelings that runs through your body
Feelings that make you feel too much
feel too much about everything

Like when a chilly feeling spread throughout your body
It gets cold inside
It gets hard to breathe
It feels unpleasant
It feels like you get consumed by the chill

Or when you're scared
and your heart beats faster
And slightest noise makes you jump
You're too scared to even breathe
It feels like you can't move

Or when you get frustrated
frustrated because of all the injustice
Then the words just pour out of you
Maybe you're so upset so you don't think before you talk
All because you want to make your voice heard
to stand up for what you believe in
Injustice creates noise in your head when you think about it
Sometimes it feels like you want to scream
scream from the top of your lungs
because of all the injustice in the world
If it would have helped to scream I would have
Instead I write and hope
Hope to influence people that way
so the injustice goes away

Sometimes you get so sad
so sad so you end up crying
Then you just want to cry
cry your eyes out

But a warm touch can lit up even the saddest face
And then a warm feeling spread throughout your body
Your tears dries away
and your lips forms a smile
You get all warm inside
Suddenly you're filled with energy
and words of joy pour out of you

So what shall one do with all the feelings
when the smallest thing make you feel like this
Maybe one should take care of oneself a little extra then
and give oneself time to relax
because it's tiresomely to feel too much
At the same time your feelings is a blessing
since your feelings make you to who you are
Without them you wouldn't be you.

Fighting Nightmares

Lying in bed
feeling tired
When nightmares ride you
you start to feel blue
Fighting to stay awake
so the devil can't take
take you down to hell

You're longing for the bell
So you can wake up from the sleep
otherwise you start to weep
It's like you're in a trap
you wish someone could give you a slap
so you can rise and shine
but it feels like you're stuck in a mine
with no way out
You want to shout
No one can hear
that you feel bad because of fear

You reach for the clock
it's like climbing a rock
You fight to open your eyes
so you finally can rise
You start to blink
it's like the missing link
because it got rid of the nightmare

Now all you have to do is dare
dare to live without letting demons haunt you
although you have no clue
how to get rid of the demons from your past
You wish they could disappear in a blast

then your mind will get peace
and you can start to feel at ease
There's a long way to go
before that happens though
All you can is do your best
then maybe your mind will get a rest

Gratefulness

When you feel gratefulness
towards life
there's no room for sadness
let go of the strife
so you can make room
for happiness
forget about the gloom
and the madness

Be grateful
Be blissful
Life is beautiful

Be grateful for water
Be grateful for electricity
Be grateful for being a daughter
Be grateful for simplicity
Be grateful for being a son
Be grateful for sun
Be grateful for those who care
Be grateful for clean air

Feel thankful
Feel wonderful
Life is colorful

Hang on

It's true what they say
that hope is the last thing
the last thing you lose

No matter how blue you feel
Hang on
soon you feel stronger
Hang on
everything will be right as rain
Hang on
because life is worth living

Even if you feel blue
Don't lose hope
because soon
a light will brighten your day
Just hang on

I'm Lost

I'm lost in a world
in a world full of darkness
I'm lost because I have no clue
no clue how to help you
how to help you get rid of your demons
I'm lost because I've seen your sad eyes
and I've heard your trembling voice

I'm lost since I don't know
don't how to help you
I'm lost because you suffer
suffer because of the demons in your past
I feel sorry
sorry that you had to be in combat
and do things
things that a normal person know nothing about
All I know is that it changed you
it changed the way you look at life

I'm lost because so many years have passed
and the shield around you has grown
grown stronger and stronger
It's like it's made of solid concrete
I'm lost since I don't know how to break through
break through your solid armor
All I know is that it must be hard to carry
hard to carry an armor made of concrete
that just grows stronger for each year that pass

I'm lost because there is a world
a world full of love and passion
I'm lost because you're not a part of it
since you're trapped
trapped inside your armor of concrete
I'm lost since I don't know which tool to use

which tool that can break through concrete
Because I want you to know that life can be wonderful
Life can be filled with butterflies and sunshine
If you just could open your armor
open it a little bit so a flower could start to grow
start to grow in that little crack
if you let the sunshine in
then soon it will start to blossom

I'm lost if you don't let the flower blossom

Jungle

Lucky me
I saw a bee
it's black and yellow
my new fellow

I followed him to his hive
where I saw a bear thrive
eating honey
it looked funny

There in the jungle
walks a Bengal
Tiger with all its beauty
protect it from all cruelty

An orangutan sits in a tree
I'm happy it's free
eating a fruit
it looks cute

Out comes an elephant
she's in her right element
She plays with her calf
it makes me laugh

I noticed a rhinoceros
he looked serious
I hope he's not afraid of me
all I want is for them to be happy and free

A butterfly follows me to my place
tears of joy rolls down my face
for me it was a pleasure
The jungle is a priceless treasure

Keep your Dreams Alive

To keep your dreams alive
is important
Because it gives you hope
hope of a brighter future

Sometimes dreams can be the only thing
the only thing that keeps you alive
Because when you're feeling blue
it soothes your mind to dream

Dream of something nice
Dream of something funny
Dream of something exciting
Dream of something wonderful

Never stop dreaming
since it keeps your hope alive
because you don't want to lose hope
So keep your dreams alive

Let go

It's hard
to let go
of something
so rare
and true

Loyal as a St Bernard
Clever as a crow
Cute as a lemming
Strong as a bear
Brave as a gnu

Remember the good
because it was right
Let go of the bad
Fill your heart with light
Don't feel blue

I'm misunderstood
Want to fight like a knight
Don't be sad
Feel bright
Love will come to you

Live Life to the Fullest

It's not cool
when people are cruel
Those who use a knife
don't appreciate life
Those who like to make fun
should be taught by a nun
how to act
so they learn to interact
with other folks
and stop make mean jokes

Cruel people aren't brave
I wonder if they were born in a cave
because it's not fun
when they use a gun
to kill
They should get a sleeping pill
so animals and nice people can feel safe
then we don't need to worry about being unsafe

Because cruel people can hurt you
some make it feel like it's taboo
to tell what you went through
I wish they knew
that their attitude
considers rude
I want to yell
that cruel people can go to hell
that's where they belong

So be strong
and don't give up
There's a way to make cruel ones shut up
Live life to the fullest

that's the coolest
way to live
then you outlive
the cruel folks
since all they have left are their mean jokes

My Meadow

I want to sit down
sit down on a meadow
on a meadow full of flowers
and forget all about
all about my sorrows for a while

I want to sit there and dream
dream about rainbows
rainbows and waterfalls
and let those beautiful
beautiful things fill my mind

I want to sit there and feel
feel the sunbeams
the sunbeams on my body
and let the sun fill me
fill me with warmth and light

I want to sit there and enjoy
enjoy the fragrance
the fragrance from the flowers
I want to sit there and dream
dream about rainbows and waterfalls
I want to sit there and feel
feel how the sunbeams
how the sunbeams kiss away
kiss away all my tears

I want to sit there
there on my meadow
and let the nature
let the nature fill me
fill me with happiness

My Treasure

The day has come to peace
I feel at ease
Out creeps the dark of night
I'm searching for a light
I notice the stars are twinkling
it's of you I'm thinking
Remembering your body near
makes me see why you are my dear
To see you is always a pleasure
because you are my treasure

High above in the sky glimmers the crescent
I know you are to me sent
from the angels in heaven above
maybe they sent my wish with a dove
Because I've been praying
and dreaming
That someone like you would find me
and never leave me

Now I'm sitting here
listen carefully so I'll be able to hear
when you come home
I wish I knew a gnome
so he could send me some magic
So our end will be classic
like in a fairyland
Where we walk through life hand in hand
so we don't fall
Because love conquers all

Never-Ending Love

I feel a never-ending love
towards animals
It's a love
that's pure and true
It's a love
that makes me happy

It tickles
when a nose sniff your face
It feels good
when you stroke an animal
feeling their velvet fur beneath your fingers
It feels nice
to give them a hug

Animals radiate such warmth
so you get all warm inside
regardless you watch them sleep
or see them make a funny move
or feel them in your arms

The love I feel for animals
makes me feel
feel like I'm walking on clouds
it makes me cheerful
It's a love that goes far beyond
far beyond worlds
because it continues
even when your companions left earth

Yes, the love I feel towards animals
is never-ending
It's a never-ending love

Once Upon a Time

Once upon a time
I had a beautiful dime
it glistened bright
in the soft moon light

A gnome grabbed my arm
told me to keep it as a lucky charm
I became glad
thanked the little lad

Who disappeared in an enchanted forest
I had a dream to become a florist
I followed in hope to see a flower
instead I found an inner power

I dared to do things I've never done
my fears were gone
I thought of my dime
Suddenly I stood under a lime

I searched my pocket
maybe a rocket
had burnt a hole
since it wasn't whole

I cried
the dime was no longer inside
should have checked before I put it in
my thoughts started to spin

It felt like tragic
because my magic
was lost
I got cold by frost

Along came a fairy
my eyes became starry
She whispered in my ear
something I needed to hear

That I had magic within
if I just believed in
myself so to speak
I felt her warmth against my cheek

I followed her to a clearing
It was spring
the dawn came fast
I no longer feared my past

She gave me strength to believe
and leave
the past behind
It gave me a peace of mind

A lucky charm is good
but know that you always should
trust yourself no matter what
and follow your gut

Pieces of Me

It's over
I wish I had a four-leaf clover
so it could bring me some luck
because I don't want to be stuck
stuck in the past
since I thought it would last

But I'm stuck
it's like I've been run over with a truck
and left are only pieces of me
I wish I was a bee
so I could fly and sting the one
the one who thought it was fun
to hurt me over and over
I wish I was a rover
then I would have taken my sword
and scared the one who thought he was a lord
I would have given the lord a mark
since all this made my mind dark
It would serve as a reminder
then maybe another time the lord would be kinder

I try to break free
so the pieces of me
can heal
so all I can feel
is harmony
and no agony

I wish I had a four-leaf clover
so I don't end up like a rover
because I don't want to be querulous
Life is too fabulous
to be stuck in the past

Time goes by fast
be sure to live in the present
so you don't get stuck in the cement

Yet I wish the lord could see
that I had the courage to break free
and what's left for the lord are only pieces
pieces of me

Precious

If you want to mend
what went wrong with your friend
Be gracious
Time is precious

Time goes by fast
leave the conflicts in the past
If you want to be considered glorious
remember time is precious

Spend time with your friend
then you confusions can fend
Don't be reckless
because time is precious

Precious are our companions
It's like onions
if we start to peel
everything becomes real
we start to cry
if we don't try
try to heal what's broken
otherwise the last words will be spoken

Don't let time pass by
if you want to avoid goodbye
So be gracious
because time is precious

Quiet

When you're tormented by a thought
you wish it could be caught
by the police
so you can get some peace
They will put it in jail
there would be no bail
There it can rot
hope it gets shot
if a fight occur
You want the thought to blur
even better if it gets killed
and grilled
Then you would sneer
because you would feel no more fear

You wish bad thoughts could be banished
so they could have vanished
away from your brain
then you would feel no more pain
You want quiet to rule
so you can keep your cool
When quiet reign
you get free from your chain
that held you back in the past
You'll be free at last
Quiet is your best friend
then your soul can be mend
you'll feel at ease
because quiet gives you inner peace

Respect Yourself

Respect yourself enough
so you walk away if something
if something bad happens

Respect yourself enough
so you walk away if someone
if someone treats you bad

Forgive yourself
let go of the past
Accept who you are
love yourself
Don't bother what people will think
do what feels right for you

Respect yourself enough
so you treat yourself with kindness
and have the courage to follow your heart

Standing Out From the Crowd

Stand up for what you believe in
even if it's hard
even if it means
means you stand out from the crowd

I know that feels lonely
but it's okay
Being alone makes you strong
strong enough
strong enough to fight for what's right

Standing out from the crowd
is courageous
It means you're brave
brave enough
brave enough to stay true to yourself

Storm

I walk along the beach
feeling sand under my feet
I look up at the sky
seeing a beautiful seagull
flying high above the sea
The sun is warm

I want my friend to reach
so I can greet
Don't want to say goodbye
I want to be your equal
I take cover under a tree
Suddenly comes a storm

I got no clue
it came from nowhere
Everything was so bright
I don't understand
how this could occur
I shed a tear

I wanted to greet you
I put on something nice to wear
You were my light
You took my hand
Everything starts to blur
I flee like a deer

Away from this city
Away from this hell
Away from the cement
Away from the cruel
Away from the dark
Away from the sadness

Don't feel pity
I was saved by the bell
An angel are to me sent
I'm not a fool
I'll always believe in the spark
From now on I choose happiness

The Angel of the Night

The angel of the night
comes to me when I go to sleep
She consoles me if I'm sad
She dries away my tears if I've cried
She makes me feel safe if I'm scared
If I wake up from a nightmare
she watch over me so I safely can fall back to sleep

The angel of the night
gives me a peace of mind
Because she brings joy
She brings kindness
She brings love
She brings calmness
She brings safety
She brings gentleness

The angel of the night
is my friend
She understands when no one else does
She communicates without words
She has a heart full of love
She is always there for me
so I can feel safe
The angel of the night
I love you

The Earth

The Earth is amazing
The mountains are a blessing
The animals are loveable
The oceans are unforgettable
The forests are wonderful
The fields are beautiful

But we must remember to take care
so we our Earth can share
with generations to come
so they can continue to pick plum
and see lions, tigers, rhinos and elephants
those magnificent giants
Otherwise they soon have vanished
I wish cruel people could be banished

We must act now
otherwise it's like we allow
that animals starts to disappear tomorrow
and that will be mankind's greatest sorrow

We must stop polluting the environment
because otherwise all we can hear is silent
Dead silence will reign
if we are insane
and let the animals, plants and oceans die
I don't want to say goodbye
to all these living beings on earth
I can't even explain how much they are worth

So we must take care of the Earth
because it gave birth
to all living creatures
which are our planet's biggest features

creatures of all different kinds
and that is mankind's
greatest pleasure
The Earth is our precious treasure

The Night

The night is my friend
It brings me peace
It consoles me
It makes me feel safe
protected from all the badness

I'm alone
but not all alone
the animals are with me
It feels pretty okay
while I'm writing these words for you

I really like the night
it's so beautiful
with all the wonderful stars
who gives you hope
The magnificent northern lights
truly amaze you with all its colors
And you can't mention the night
without talking about the moon
the gorgeous, mystical moon
that you never can get enough of

I'm sitting here now
looking out through the window
The soil is all covered
in a thick layer of soft snow

A little snowflake glitters
It makes me hopeful
that something so tiny
can shine so bright
It's like a miracle

And now it's a season for miracles
Christmas is just around the corner
and if you look closely
you might see an angel
flying above you in the sky

No matter what season it is
miracles do happen
every now and then
You just need to believe in them
and when you least expect it
it will happen
That one special thing you always dreamed about
Just keep up your spirit

And in the meanwhile
let the night surround you with all its magic

There are No Words

There are no words for what you are feeling now
The tears are rolling down your cheeks
like an endless stream
Eventually they will stop
but not the pain in your heart

You'll keep asking yourself why
why did this have to happen
I'm sorry my dear friend
no one has the answer to that
Sometimes the fate is cruel
and there is nothing we can do to change that
I wish one could change the fate sometimes
but I guess everything happens for a reason
And that is something that is very hard to understand
Personally I don't understand why cruel things happens to your beloved ones
That is a question that never will get answered

Your heart is bleeding now
and so it will for a long time ahead
In the meanwhile
Remember that you gave your friends a home when no one else did
That you gave them love
which they wouldn't have gotten if it wasn't for you
Please know that you filled their hearts with joy
I am convinced that they felt all the love you had for them

Now they are jumping around
from one cloud to another
They will look down at you

and see your sad face
They wish that they could tell you to not be sad
that they are okay
They want to tell you that you will meet them again
when your time is come

In the meanwhile they want to see you smile again
They want you to look up at the sky and wave
then they will wave back in their own special way
There are no words for what you are feeling now
but eventually time will heal your heart
It's hard to believe now
but it will

Thinking of You

The sky is blue
like a forget-me-not
The sun is yellow
like a butterbur
The angels in heaven are white
like catnip

I'm thinking of you
please forget me not
You're sturdy as a willow
I don't want our memories to blur
It's night
I'm on a ship

The ocean is blue
I'm thinking of you
The stars are yellow
I wish to be sturdy as a willow
The steering wheel is white
I know we are right

Thou shalt Not Kill

Thou shalt not kill
is one of God's commandments

We celebrate Christmas in memory of God's son,
but why does millions of animals have to die because of that
Why celebrate his son by killing innocent creatures
when God said:
Thou shalt not kill

I think that all creatures should be included in those words
regardless if it's human beings
or creatures in the sea
or creatures on the land
Because all living beings have a right to live
they have the right to live for their own sake

And Christmas is a season of love and joy
So why does so many creatures have to die
Why does they have to pay with their life
when people celebrate God's son
A God who said:
Thou shalt not kill

To Me They are All the Same

What shall one do
when one's heart is full of sadness
My mother, our cats, our dogs
Our cows, our heifers, our bulls
Our goat, our sheep, our ducks
Our rabbits, our guinea pigs, our budgies
Our fish, our hens, our roosters
All these creatures have come and gone
during the years I spent here on earth
I loved them all
That's why my heart is full of sadness

My cat was the last one to leave me
He left me for a better place
I miss him
I miss them all
I miss them so much it hurts inside
It can be anything that reminds me of them
like the summer landscape
Now they are all gone
It hurts

Lots of people don't understand
how one can feel bad when a pet has died
They say it is just a pet
But they are wrong, it is not just a pet
It's a family member, a close friend

What's even harder for people to understand
is when you cry over a cow
To me they are all the same
A cow, a cat, a bull, a heifer
A budgie, a goat, a rabbit, a chicken

A dog, a duck, a guinea pig, a fish
I make no difference
To me they are all family members

I wish that all people could open their eyes and see
See that the eyes of a bull
are just as beautiful as the eyes of a dog
But maybe people are afraid
afraid to look into the eyes of a bull
Because then they would see that they have a soul
That they want to live and not become food
I hope that one day people wake up
and realize what they are doing to the animals

In the meantime I let the cat I have left console me
I know she will help me to live
Help me to live with all the grief I carry in my heart
I use to look into her beautiful eyes
Then she blinks and so do I
I can tell by her look that she understands me
because we're both grieving
She lost her soul mate
and I lost my beloved friend
She blinks
I blink
We're connected forever

True Friendship

What's the meaning of a true friend

For me that's someone who is always there for you
Someone that lifts you up when you are down
Someone that makes the tears stop rolling down your cheeks
and put a smile on your face instead
Someone who are there for you through bad times
and makes those times feel less scary and lonely
Someone who are there for you through good times
to share your laughter with
Someone you can share your problems with
without feeling stupid
Someone you dare to be crazy with
and not being judged by that
Someone who listens
when no one else will

I have a true friend like that
Who consoles me when I'm sad
Who makes my sorrows go away
by telling me a silly joke
Who helps me breathe
by listening to my words
Who turns up when I least expect it
and make me laugh
Who is with me in spirit
to make me feel less lonely

No matter what silly things I tell him
he's still there the next day
that makes me feel safe

Even if I feel like a crazy girl at times
he's still there for me

I don't know what I have done to deserve a friend like this
But maybe someone saw that I needed some guiding
to help me see the light in the end of the tunnel
And sent me this friendship
like a blessing from heaven above

There are no words for a true friend like this
Maybe he was a knight in an earlier life
who saved fair ladies and kissed their hands
He sure reminds me of one

Maybe he is an angel sent down to help me
because there is something elvish about him
An aura that feels like magic
since being in his presence makes me feel euphoric

I'm truly blessed with a friend like this
who sends me his magic
to watch over me while I sleep

Underneath the Stars

I live my life underneath the stars
underneath a star-spangled sky
The full moon gives a soft light
the snowflakes glisten

The snow covers the soil
covers it in a thick layer
The hills look soft
underneath the star-spangled sky

I walk on the moonlit snow crust
a snow crust that carry me
wherever I want to go
I admire the view on top of a hill
where I see a shooting star
I make a wish

I live my life underneath the stars
underneath a star-spangled sky
among shooting stars and sparkling snowflakes
While I'm hoping my wish
hoping my wish come true
I live my life underneath the stars

Vacation

Close your eyes and imagine
You stand next to a jasmine
breathe in the heavenly fragrance
enjoy the silence
no noise
that annoys

Birds are singing
and you hear church bells ringing
far away
Below is a sage-green bay
you decide to take a dip
Later you sip
on a drink
while you think

Sitting on the beach
eating a ripe peach
The sky is blue
a sea gull lands next to you
You look up at heaven
feels like you're in seventh heaven

You go for a walk
in the distance you see a hawk
it shrieks
You admire the mountain peaks
Wandering over hills
Nature fills
you with pleasure
This day dream is your own treasure

Going for a vacation
doesn't mean you have to leave the nation

You can go for free in your mind
then you'll find
the greatest place of all
big or small
Maybe you meet a gnome
who takes you to the green hills of home

There's no place like fairyland
just grab your special somebody's hand
and walk over hills and across streams
let the sunbeams
kiss you dry

Give it a try
then you'll see
that you can go to the sea
any time you like
and go for a hike

Just close your eyes
and let the butterflies
bring you to fairyland
hand in hand
with the one you call your dear
then you'll only music hear

Walking on Clouds

If I could
I would have
If I could bring you back to life
I would have
If taken my life would have brought you back
I would have
But I know that's not the case
if I die won't make you alive again

But oh, how I wish, that you were still alive
Oh, how I wish, that you still walked on earth
side by side with me
Oh, how I wish, that I still could hear you breathe
breathe next to me
Oh, how I wish, that I still could look into your eyes
your beautiful, warm, wise, kind eyes
Oh, how I wish, that you were still by my side
so I could give you a hug

What I wouldn't give to feel your body
feel your body in my arms again
Because it made me feel safe and happy
to feel your heartbeat
What I wouldn't give if I only
if I only could make all the wrongs right
What I wouldn't give to see you
to see you just once more
Oh, how I wish, that you were still alive

But I know you're walking on clouds now
that you're fine among the angels
I know that I have to wait until we can meet

I know you'll be there waiting when I see the light
I guess everything happens for a reason
but why you had to die I will never understand
I know that I must keep on living
but oh how it hurts
since you're no longer by my side

I know you're fine up there
up there among the angels
But still it hurts to be left alone
alone walking on earth
I dream of the day when I'll walk
walk on clouds
walk on the clouds with you
Because then we'll be united forever
and nothing can ever break us apart again
A piece of me is already walking
walking on the clouds with you
Because a part of my heart is always with you

There are different kinds of loves
the love I felt for you are that special one
that kind of love that never dies
That kind of love that goes far beyond worlds
because it's so pure and powerful
That kind of love doesn't last for a lifetime
no, it lasts for eternity
because it's so deep and true
That kind of love never dies
no, it lasts forever
It keeps living in your heart
even when your darling is gone
gone to another world

But darling, oh, how I wish
Oh, how I wish, that you were still by my side
so I could give you a hug

What is love?

What is love
This little word, only four letters long
yet so powerful
You can't touch it because it's not a physical thing
yet you know it exists

But what is love
Is it love when you think of your dead mother
and you can hear inside you what she would have said if she could
Is it love if you do things that you know she would have loved

You never know what little thing will turn your feelings in motion
when someone close to you has died
These little things can be
a commercial
a picture
a memory
a fruit
a movie
a treadmill
Yes you never know which thing will make you blue
when someone you cared about is gone forever

Is it love or grief when your eyes get teary by these small things
Things that mean nothing to others but the world to you
Maybe it's grief since you lost someone
Or is it love you're feeling
since these little things make you feel so much

I try to believe that everything happens for a reason
but that's difficult at times
Because I can't understand why my mother had to die all of
a sudden
It felt like my world turned upside down
I was left alone with all the feelings
Feelings that make you feel too much
Once in a while it feels like a storm is going on inside my
heart

I thank God that he sent me an angel to help me get through
this
An angel that my mother met briefly before she went to
heaven
I believe that angels comes in different shapes
Like a cat purring in your lap
Or a friend who spends time with you
Or just a feeling of peace inside you

But what is love
I believe angels are love
So maybe love actually is a physical thing
Or is it just a feeling
Who knows
But I do know that angels are both visible and invisible
You never know where angels are
If someone will turn up next to you when you least expect it
Or if it just flies above your head right at this moment
to protect you from all the danger

Although love is a wonderful thing it also hurts
Soon it's Holiday season and it will hurt when I see all the
Christmas lights
because that was the last thing I talked with my mother
about
I miss you mom

Whisper in the Night

Feeling sad
dreaming of a fairy
hoping she can throw
throw fairy dust over me
Away goes all my heartache
and misery
like a whisper in the night

She whispers to me
that all I have to do
is believe
believe in myself
trust my gut
eventually time will heal
heal my broken heart
and bewildered soul

A seed is planted
I just need to nurture it
so it can grow
grow gutsy and powerful
I just need to persevere
persevere through all misery
Believing brighter days
will come my way
like a whisper in the night

Xmas

Sometimes I wonder
wonder if everyone knows
why we celebrate Xmas
It seems for many
that the number of gifts are most important
Everyone is in a hurry
hurry to make everything look good
look good on the outside
They're too busy so they forget
forget about the inner peace

Sometimes I wonder
wonder how many cares
what Xmas is all about
I believe the world would be
would be a better place
if people cared more about
the inside than the outside
and cared more about
their behavior towards others

Sometimes I wonder
wonder how many remember
who's birthday we celebrate
A man who spread love
Love, kindness and joy
during his short time on earth

Xmas should be about love
and no egomania
Xmas should be about kindness
and no evil-mindedness
Xmas should be about joy
and no drama

Xmas should be about
finding inner peace
That's what Christmas is all about

You

It has always been You
You're the one
the one I've been waiting
waiting all my life for

You turned up from nowhere
like the sun after a rainy day
You made me bloom
like when coltsfoots open up
open up to sunbeams

You're like a sunbeam
that lights up the day
and make all the sorrows go away
You're the light
that banish the darkness

You're the star
the brightest star in my life
Your aura shines so bright
it makes me feel
feel euphoric in your presence

Your warmth is like magic
magic to me
because it makes me high
high on love

Yes, it has always been You
You're the one
the one I chose to give
give my heart to
I'm yours
yours forever

Your own Best Friend

Lying in bed
Beaming
Thinking

Thinking of all you've accomplished
during the day
during your life

Be satisfied
feel satisfied
with being you

At the end of the day
all you have is you
So be your own best friend

Your Special Someone

Walking along a stream
birds are singing
Sitting down on a rock
dreaming of your special someone

Beam
Wonder what the one are bringing
Checking the clock
soon comes the one

The one brings strawberries and cream
You're listening
Murmuring water below the rock
You're having fun

Feeling the steam
Kissing and hugging
emotions unlock
Before you had to let the one run

But now you're a team
laughing and dancing
on a solid rock
The one who ran is now your sun

Zero

When you hit rock bottom
it feels like below zero
since everything feels
Sad
Cold
Hard
Dark
Lonely
Empty

You start to wonder
wonder if you ended up in hell
since you're covered
covered in darkness
You feel trapped
trapped like in a prison
with no way out

Suddenly you see a crack
a crack in the darkness
A light that flickers
but soon it gets steady
because you start to believe
believe in yourself

You decide to escape
You grab a ladder
and start climbing
climbing towards the light
because you start to realize
realize that you're precious

Finally you're on a meadow
a meadow full of flowers
flowers and butterflies
You're surrounded with light
and gone is the darkness

Then you realize you're a hero
because you went from zero
from zero to your own hero
since you had the wisdom to see
see that you're precious
And you had the courage
the courage to believe
believe in yourself

www.ingramcontent.com/pod-product-compliance
Lightning Source LLC
Chambersburg PA
CBHW071330040426
42444CB00009B/2122